I Can Be Me

A Helping Book for Children of Alcoholic Parents

Dianne S. O'Connor, Ed.D.

authorHOUSE®

AuthorHouse™
1663 Liberty Drive
Bloomington, IN 47403
www.authorhouse.com
Phone: 1-800-839-8640

First published by AuthorHouse 10/9/2009

ISBN: 978-1-4259-9899-8 (sc)

Printed in the United States of America
Bloomington, Indiana

This book is printed on acid-free paper.

Fourth printing

Table of Contents

Introduction

I Can Be Me, A Helping Book, educates and supports children growing up with addicted family members. Children can suffer whether the addicted family member is a parent, sibling or other close relative.

Children often need help both during the family member's phase of active drug abuse and through their struggle for recovery.

Core Topics

Chapter 1 – Can't stop – focuses on the basics, teaching children about addiction and introducing some common experiences and feelings that children of chemical abusers share. Children learn they cannot cause or stop the addiction.

Chapter 2 – Feelings – focuses further on the typical feelings of such children and encourages them to acknowledge and cope with their own.

Chapter 3 – Feeling Masks – addresses the defenses we use to hide our true feelings and encourages children to find times when they can lower their defenses, relax and be themselves.

Chapter 4 – A Family Problem – teaches about the repercussions a family member's addiction can have on all family members while validating children's typical reactions and encouraging them to adopt healthy coping behaviors of their own.

Chapter 5 – Help Yourself – teaches children to focus on themselves, to take care of themselves and to move toward more rewarding lives, despite the family problem of addiction.

Chapter 6 – Decisions – focuses on the need to make good decisions and provides a framework for helping children to develop sound decision-making skills.

Chapter 7 – Family Change – helps children to acknowledge the good things about their families and encourages them to build on these positive aspects.

Chapter 8 – Lots of Kids Like Us – stresses that children are not alone and that there are many others who share their problem and many places to find help. This chapter encourages children to break through their isolation and to obtain help, camaraderie and fun.

Children At Risk

To cope with the stress of their family lives, children of the chemically dependent often adopt behaviors which predispose them to addiction, abusive and/or addicted marriage partners and various other mental health problems.

They experience difficulty developing healthy, close relationships, have trouble expressing feelings and often suffer from low self-esteem.

They are more apt to know the pain and trauma that society strives to help children cope with, such as divorce, suicide, physical and sexual abuse.

In schools their problems often surface as behavioral and learning difficulties. Statistics indicate that these children are over represented among those who pass through our mental health facilities, courts, prisons and the juvenile justice system.

While many such children appear to cope successfully as they adopt achievement oriented and approval-seeking behaviors, they often do so at great cost to themselves. The living problems they experience go unnoticed.

Forgotten Children

Society generally ignores these children, even though they face up to four times the risk of becoming chemically dependent. They are an undetected, rarely helped population. And great numbers of them exist. In a classroom of 25, it is estimated that four to six children live in homes where familial addiction is a problem. One out of six families must cope with the addiction of one of its members.

Addiction is a number one health problem exceeding both heart disease and cancer in impact. Its destructive effects spread well beyond the addicted individual to include not only the larger society but family members including the youngest of children.

It is essential that parents, caring adults and helping professionals focus on the plight of these children. They must develop an awareness of their issues and the strategies and skills to help them. Such children have been untreated, misdiagnosed and ignored too long.

Early Intervention

Preventive programs should begin early with these high risk children. By four or five, many have adopted unhealthy coping patterns to deal with the stress of living with an addicted parent. The longer the child depends on these coping patterns the harder they will be to reverse.

With research indicating that children make decisions about using drugs in grades 5 to 8, the urgency to begin early prevention programs is great, especially with these children. A commitment to prevention must focus directly upon these children, their parents and other significant adults in their lives. Otherwise the intergenerational cycle of addiction will continue unchecked.

Why This Book?

This book is designed to meet the needs of professionals and parents, who want a simple, inexpensive, yet comprehensive resource that they can easily implement to help young children. At the heart of this program is the belief that children can learn to cope with problems they understand and move toward a healthier balanced development.

With this book adults can reach children early before unhealthy coping patterns become deeply ingrained, before children meet strong peer pressure to try drugs and during an age when significant adults have the most influence.

Format

I Can Be Me provides knowledge and emotional support within a framework of eight core topics. It covers the pertinent issues that need to be addressed with these children; it teaches them about addiction and its familial effects while focusing on the universal feelings and concerns they share. This book encourages children to express their feelings while providing the framework to point them in a healthier direction.

Goals

The four main goals of this book are:

1. To teach children about addiction and its familial effects.
2. To help them understand and cope with their feelings.
3. To let children know that they are not alone, others share their problems and there are places where they can find assistance.
4. To guide children toward healthier personal outlooks and coping skills.

Suggested Use

Children's Support Groups

- As the core resource around which to build a support group.

- As a supplemental resource within an already established program.

- As a copy given to families to help introduce parents to the issues their children face and to serve as a support tool for children after the group has ended.

Counseling And Therapy Programs

- As an educational tool to bring the issues these children face to greater awareness, thereby facilitating their address during the counseling session.

- As a catalyst to encourage the expression and validation of feelings.

- As a guide to help determine the individual needs of each child.

Addiction Treatment Programs

- As a resource to share with parents, to help them understand their children's issues and to learn how they can help.

- As a guide to treatment center staff working with young children.

Parents And Other Caring Adults

- As a guide to parents, who are a vital link in reaching these children because they can provide the consistency and daily reshaping of family interactions.

School Systems

- As a guide for support staff who counsel children and their families.

- As a resource for children, one which should be available to them in the school library or as part of their classroom book collection.

- As a book to be read and discussed with children, perhaps as part of a larger unit on family studies or drug education.

Community Awareness

- As a means for family physicians, pediatricians, psychiatrists, psychologists, educators, social workers, librarians, the clergy and all others who come in contact with young children and families to raise awareness about this issue, by including resources, such as *I Can Be Me*, within their libraries, waiting rooms, offices and classrooms.

How to Implement

Reducing Isolation

The illustrations that relate to children's experiences and feelings are based on true accounts expressed by children through their art and discussion. When children understand that their feelings and experiences are shared by others, they will feel less alone and will be more accepting of their own feelings and of themselves.

Expressing Feelings

I Can Be Me encourages children to acknowledge and express their feelings. Of equal importance is to hear others reveal and acknowledge theirs. Children will hear others who share similar experiences speak to them through the pages of this book. As they identify with these feelings and concerns, children will reveal and accept their own.

The Reticent Child

Some children will remain reluctant to reveal their emotions and worries. They should never be forced to do so. However, these children can still be helped. Just knowing what the problem is, that they are not alone and that they did not cause and cannot stop the addiction can provide tremendous relief. In addition, they learn help is available and may be more open to help in the future.

Art Format

While the art format may seem repetitious, drawing often eases the release of pent up feelings, and is an especially useful tool with these children who frequently deny their emotions and concerns.

Drawing also allows for the healthy release of feelings. Again, this is useful with these children who frequently ventilate feelings inappropriately.

Further, the concrete example of a pictured feeling or experience helps children verbalize issues that they might otherwise have difficulty expressing. Those children who are reluctant to discuss their issues are often quite the opposite with their drawings and eager to share them with others.

Children are not expected to draw pictures about every issue but only those that have special meaning or that the counselor feels are most pertinent. However, some children may prefer not to draw but instead to write about or discuss their concerns.

Age Range

The format is designed for children from age 4 to 12. Both the pictures and shorter text that accompany them serve as discussion starters with young children; the longer text is aimed at the older child.

Other Family Problems

This book can be used with children who are experiencing other family problems. You can say:

1. Parental addiction is one family problem some children have.
2. Families have other troubles and children often feel and act the same way whatever the family problem.
3. The book discusses parallels and differences between children's particular problems, feelings and experiences and those pictured and discussed in the book.

Special Note To Parents

Due to the family patterns of isolation and lack of communication, especially about feelings, which have frequently developed through the years, your children may be reluctant to share their feelings and concerns. It is all too new and they are still fearful.

Just reading and discussing this book can provide much relief but it also offers children the option of being alone and drawing or writing about issues (perhaps using an invisible pen, talking into a tape recorder or writing in their own private diary). When they feel more comfortable, they will begin to share their issues with you.

Groups Or Individuals

This book is designed for use with groups or individuals. Although group sessions are important, individual sessions can be of great benefit to these children.

Due to the preoccupation of addicted people with their drug and of other family members with the addicted person and their own hurt and pain, children seldom receive focused attention from the primary adults in their lives.

Sharing this book with a caring adult can provide this focused attention, reducing children's isolation and teaching them that they are valued and worthy of attention.

Introducing I Can Be Me

Some things you might say include:

1. All families have problems. This book is about the family problem of addiction.
2. You will learn about drug addiction and what happens in families when someone takes too much of a harmful drug.

3. This book is called *I Can Be Me* because even when a family member is addicted to drugs, children can learn to take good care of themselves and lead happier lives.
4. Many of the pictures in this book are about real things that happened to real children who live in families where someone has the problem of addiction.
5. You might want to share your own feelings and experiences just like the children whose experiences and ideas are drawn in this book.
6. You can use your own markers and paper to draw and write about the ideas in this book.
7. No one will discuss or show another person what you talk, write or draw about unless you say "It's okay".

Caution: Give children only one marker to use. Otherwise some may spend all their time coloring and avoid expressing their issues. Some children become inhibited, believing they must draw perfect pictures. Stress that the ideas are important, not superior artwork. Other children may try to copy the book's drawings. For most children it is best to close the book while they draw.

Levels of Intervention

1. **Education.** This book teaches children about addiction and its familial effects and shows how children can help themselves. Children learn that they are not alone and they did not cause and cannot stop the addiction.
2. **Expression And The Validation Of Feelings.** This book validates children's feelings, presenting them as understandable and common to other children who share the problem of familial addiction. In addition, children are encouraged to share their feelings through art, discussion and writing.

3. **Skill Development And Reshaping Behavior.** Children's expressions of feelings, experiences and worries will suggest appropriate intervention strategies.

What To Do

1. **Read and Discuss.** Read this book through and familiarize yourself with the concepts addressed. Then share this book – a chapter at a time – with the children, expressing your own feelings and experiences and encouraging them to express theirs.

To promote discussion you might ask:

- Have you ever felt this way?

- Have you ever had a similar experience?

- Do you know others who have?

- How do you think they felt?

- Why do you think they felt this way?

2. **Deal With Feelings.** Encourage the child to choose a picture to draw, write about or discuss, or the adult can select one she feels it is important for the child to address. Validate the child's feelings by saying some of the following:

- How do you feel?

- That makes sense to me.

- I can understand that.

- Others feel that way too.

- You feel/felt sad or happy or angry.

Never say:

- You shouldn't feel that way.

- You don't feel that way.

3. **Develop New Skills.** What you learn from the child's art, writing and discussion can lead to intervention strategies to support the child.

Examples

1. Through his drawings one child expressed love for and a desire to be closer to an older sister. Strategies were developed to strengthen this bond.
2. Another child expressed anger toward a drug abusing parent and recognized that he often expressed this anger through bullying younger children. This child needed guidance to help him handle his anger appropriately and develop healthier interactions with others.
3. The Whole Wheel in Chapter 5 is used to assess the child's strengths and weaknesses and determine the areas that need to be developed if the child is to move toward a healthy balanced development.
4. Similarly, thinking about children in terms of the roles they play (see Chapter 4) can suggest strategies to help children break out of these roles and lower their typical defenses.

5. Social skills need to be taught to these children, often with direct intervention. The children seldom observe adults engaged in healthy, human interactions. Chapter 8 is designed to assess the social strengths and needs of each child. The sociogram, included in this chapter, can help determine who is important to the child and where to build and develop relationships.

Go Easy!

Pushing the child socially too soon can backfire. The child often lacks both the confidence and skills to fit easily into a group and if pushed too soon, may be ostracized and ridiculed by the others. Many children need time to build self-esteem, to be a good friend to themselves and to establish a positive caring relationship with an adult who can teach them their value. However, with careful planning positive social interactions can be arranged. These, in turn, will enhance the child's self-esteem.

A Word About Self-Esteem

Positive self-esteem is crucial to improving the lives of these children. Poor self-esteem is a common trait of the addicted and of those with various other mental health problems. Adults working with these children must do their utmost to enhance the child's self-esteem and proceed with this quest long after working through this book. Refer to the many books on the market for help.

How I Can Be Me Encourages Self-Esteem

- by teaching children they are not alone, that they are not strange, they share the same feelings and experiences as others.

- by easing children's guilt and letting them know they are not responsible for the addiction.
- by validating children's feelings.
- by teaching children they are special, valued people who deserve good treatment.
- by helping children to acknowledge their own strengths and to be positive about their families and each family member.
- by teaching children that they have control over their own lives and responsibility for their decisions.
- by providing focused attention for children as they work through this book with an adult.
- by helping children to trust their perceptions.
- by encouraging children toward a balanced development so that all of their being can flourish and grow.

The Role of Parents

Parents can steer their children toward a healthier balanced development and improve family interactions.

Change For The Better

Think about the characteristics of troubled families, some of which are listed in Chapter 4. Do any typify your family? What changes would you like to make? Begin making these changes so that family life can become a happier, more rewarding experience for your children.

Think about your family of origin. Remember the positives and build on those with your own children. Think about the negatives that you may be repeating, then take steps to stop. For example, focus upon feelings (use the feeling lists in Chapter 2 to help you). How were feelings expressed in your childhood family? What feelings were most often expressed? What feelings were rarely or never expressed? How do you wish it could have been? What patterns are you repeating in the present? What changes could you make to help your own children?

You could also think about improving communication and building closeness. There are a number of ways of doing this. One is to focus on feelings by:

- paying attention to your own feelings and modeling the healthy expression of these when appropriate.
- accepting and acknowledging the feelings of your children (see the earlier section on Dealing With Feelings).
- talking about hard-to-share feelings. You could encourage your children to share a time when they had one of these feelings (use the chart at the end of Chapter 2 for help). Don't force your children to share if they don't wish to.
- sharing experiences with your children, talking to them about your day and encouraging them to do the same.
- thinking about and discussing both comfortable and uncomfortable feelings.

To facilitate the sharing of feelings use the chart at the end of Chapter 2. Each family member could choose one of these feelings and share a time when he experienced that feeling, either during that week, day or when someone was using drugs.

Remember all feelings are okay. Accept and don't judge these feelings. You may like to tell your children about times when you had similar feelings.

Another way of building closeness in your family is to share fun times together. Why not try:

- making a list of family times you have enjoyed.
- making a list of family fun you would like to enjoy.

- choosing one thing from either of these lists to do this week.
- playing some cooperative games to provide children with models of family members working together cooperatively to achieve a common goal.
- setting aside a time each week to be together and enjoy each other.

Many families have found it useful to plan weekly family meetings. Let each family member voice his issues and concerns (from the mundane such as family chores to planning a family vacation). Or discuss the events of the week – how they felt about them; what they would like to change. Give children a vote and a sense of control over their lives. Accept their opinions and ideas.

Preventive Strategies

Neil Panzica (1983) suggests that families who wish to take preventive steps to "stack the cards against drug abuse" should work toward some of the following family patterns:

1) **A focus on the value of work and responsibility** where children have chores, responsibilities and money is earned through neighborhood jobs (e.g. babysitting).
2) **Discipline, curfews, rules** that set clear, reasonable limits and provide caring supervision, yet avoid harsh and frequent punishment.
3) **Extracurricular activities** that encourage children to pursue their interests and strengths.
4) **Restricted TV viewing** because too much television viewing increases isolation in families and inhibits communication. Also television can serve as an escape and become a dependency, or addiction in itself and programs often model non-feeling, abusive behavior (both verbal and physical violence).

5) **Developing good parenting characteristics** like being a good listener who communicates pride in his/her children. Consult children on family decisions but don't let their needs over-rule yours; be firm for those issues that require that parents have the final say. Also being affectionate, warm parents who laugh, have family fun and a sense of humor.

6) **In addition work toward consistency** with regular bedtimes, meals, parenting behavior and clear, consistent rules. Also work toward a flexible, caring approach that is not rigid and controlling and reduce isolation through the following measures:

- involvement in the community.
- encouraging children to bring friends home and join after school activities.
- increasing interaction with each other (healthy expression of feelings and conflict resolution as well as family fun).

Don't pressure kids to take sides during parental disputes and remember to comfort children when there are problems – don't cover up or deny them.

Most Important

It is important to provide a healthy role model for your children. Get help for and take good care of yourself. Model healthy self-expression of your own feelings and ideas and positive self-esteem. Children identify with and model their own behavior upon those of the significant adults in their lives. Strive toward a healthy balanced development of your own. Use the Whole Wheel chart in Chapter 5 for help.

Provide your child with focused attention: a time (even 10 minutes per day) when you attend to your child, showing an interest in his feelings, experiences and thoughts, share a story or game together. Parental interest teaches your child that he is a valued person, worthy of your time and attention, that you care for him and enjoy his company. This will build his confidence and self-esteem.

Thinking About The Child

Use the section on roles in Chapter 4 to think about the roles your child may be playing. While these roles suggest various strengths children may nevertheless invest too much of themselves in a role. When this happens they hide themselves and fail to develop their true potential. Again, use the Whole Wheel chart, chapter 5, to think about the areas your child might be neglecting. Provide him/her with opportunities and encouragement to develop these neglected areas.

Don't discourage the healthier qualities inherent to these roles. The hero can be responsible and compassionate, while the lost child is often creative and independent. The scapegoat can be honest and gutsy, the clown funny and amusing. Encourage these positive qualities, but also help the child transcend these roles. Remember these roles are not distinct. Children often demonstrate various characteristics from each.

The Controller/Family Hero/Caretaker

To help this child:
- spread responsibility.
- repeat "you do not have to be responsible for...,"
- repeat "you are not responsible for my feelings..."
- encourage them to relax and have fun to break their obsession with work and over-achievement.
- help them to lean on others, express their needs, weakness and pain and accept failure.

- help them to feel worthwhile for who they are, not solely because of their accomplishments.

The Fighter-Scapegoat/Angry One

To help this child:
- remember self-esteem is often low because he has been labeled the "bad guy" and thus has received little positive feedback.
- helping him discover that the addiction is the problem, not some problem within himself, can provide great relief.
- the caring and concern of a significant adult can enhance self-esteem.
- help him find healthy outlets for his anger.
- encourage him to express his fears and problems as well as his successes.
- remember this child may need professional help if he has turned to delinquency, drug abuse or any other self-destructive behavior.

Adjuster/Lost Child

This child:
- needs a great deal of patience to draw her out.
- needs to feel safe with another before she can begin expressing herself.
- often is in need of individual attention and is easily overshadowed by others in a group.
- needs help in building closer relationships, beginning first with you as a caring adult.
- needs to be encouraged in peer relationships and to join groups (don't push her before she is ready).
- needs to be encouraged to express her wants and needs.
- needs to be taught healthy ways to resolve conflict (e.g., assertiveness skills).

- needs a sense of control, a feeling that she can shape her own life.
- needs praise of the positive (e.g., her creativity and independence).

Mascot/Clown

This child needs:

- to be encouraged to take himself seriously to make decisions, accept responsibility and express his own ideas and feelings.
- to be taught organizational skills, how to complete projects and how to solve problems. He should be asked frequently "What do you think, need?" to get in touch with his feelings.
- help to feel good because of his own accomplishments not as a result of others' approval (e.g., say, "You must be proud of yourself", when he meets with success).

A Final Word

This book can provide education and relief for the child, which is a first step toward change. It is not viewed as a one shot program or a cure-all for these children but is instead seen as a catalyst to promote healthy ongoing change in the child's life.

1

Can't Stop

Drugs

Some drugs can help us get better if we take the right amount

We can find drugs in many places. Some are in the medicine cabinet or the drugstore.

These drugs affect our bodies and help them to heal when we are hurt or sick.

Write the names of some drugs that help us feel better.

_____

_____

_____

But remember, even a drug that can help us can hurt us if we take too much.

Too much of a healing drug can poison our bodies and make us sick.

There are other drugs that are harmful even when people take a little bit.

These drugs affect how our brains work, and how people think and feel. They are found in many different things people take.

Nicotine is a harmful drug found in cigarettes.

Alcohol is a drug found in many drinks like beer, scotch, whiskey, vodka and gin. Alcohol can be harmful when people drink too much.

Pot is the nickname for marijuana, another harmful drug, which hurts people's brains and changes the way they think and feel.

Other harmful drugs include heroin, cocaine and LSD.

Some drugs harm us even if we take a little bit. They hurt people's brains so that they think and act in strange ways.

Write the names of any harmful drugs you know about.

_____

_____

_____

What Happens?

When people take too much of an alcoholic drink like beer, whiskey or wine, they become "drunk". When they take too much of a harmful drug like marijuana or cocaine, we say they are "high".

Drunk or high people act strange. This is because the drug hurts the brain and the body no longer works properly.

Drunk or high people might forget things or act clumsily and fall down.

Sometimes they act angry, scary and mean or even crazy and then they fall asleep.

Look at the balloons below. **Draw** a string to the balloons that tell how a drunk or high person you know acted.

Once when my dad got drunk, he put his pipe in his mouth upside down and walked around thinking he was smoking it.

Can I Cause The Drinking?

Sometimes children think it is their fault when a family member is addicted. But this is never true. Children do not cause parents to drink or take drugs.

Why do you think some children think that the drug taking is their fault?

Draw or write about it.

Have you ever felt this way?

Maybe if I was good and did the right thing, my mom wouldn't drink so much.

Stuck To A Drug

Many children think they can stop the drinking or drug taking but they can't. The person who takes too much alcohol or drugs is addicted. Addicted means "stuck".

Addicted people might want to stop the drinking or drug taking. But it is a habit most find hard to stop even when they try very hard. Addicted people are stuck to their drug just as bubble gum sticks to your shoe.

Not everyone who takes an alcoholic drink is addicted. Only those who get stuck and can't stop.

What do you find hard to stop?

Chewing Pencils

Chewing Nails

Licking Ice Cream Cones

An Addicted Person

Sometimes it is hard to like addicted people. At times they seem mean and bad. The drugs affect their body and brain. It is as if their body doesn't work properly.

They can't be themselves. The drug gets in the way of their love. They forget to treat people in a caring way.

But addicted people can get better if they decide to and ask for the help they need.

Addicted people can be anybody – teachers,
doctors, dancers, mechanics or policemen.

Once they start taking their drugs,
they can't stop.

They have a problem but they can
decide to get help.

Children Can't Stop The Drug Taking!

Addiction is a problem children can't cause or stop. They can't make the addicted person better. Doctors and other people who know about addiction can help the addicted person.

Addicted people must decide to get better and get the help they need. Children can't do it for them.

Sometimes children might try to stop the drinking or drug-taking.

Have you ever done this?

Draw a picture about it.

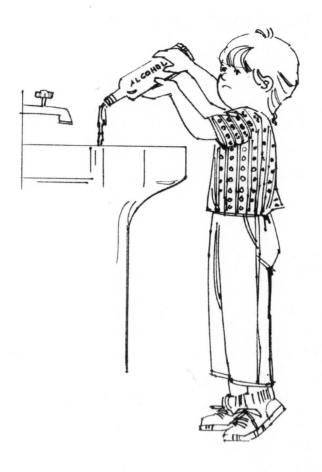

I find where my dad hides his bottles and I pour them all out.

Living With An Addicted Person Isn't Always Fun

Sometimes addicted people don't notice the children.

They don't play with them or help them or really listen to them when they speak. Their body is there but it seems like they aren't inside.

I feel small and all alone, as if I don't matter.

Children want to make addicted people stop taking their drugs. It isn't much fun living in a family where people get drunk or high.

Drunk or high people act strange. They seem out of control and sometimes they scare and embarrass children.

Draw a picture of how children might feel when around a drunk or high person.

No one laughs and everyone is worried.
I feel scared when everyone yells.

Addicted People Change A Lot

They act like different people, and you don't always know how they'll behave.

Sometimes they act like people we don't like.

Sometimes they act as if they don't like us.

Sometimes they are nice and treat us well.

Other times they seem mean.

All of this change is very confusing.

Draw a picture of an addicted person who changes a lot.

How do children feel when this happens?

Mad/Angry   Happy/Kind

Picture inspired by a child's drawing in My Dad Loves Me, My Dad Has A Disease by Claudia Black.

Ugly Words

The addicted person often acts mad at others.

People who take drugs or drink too much alcohol sometimes have difficulty managing their emotions, especially anger.

When they get angry, they may be angry at something or someone else and take out their anger on others.

They get mad and can be unkind and cruel to others.

Children don't deserve to be hurt even with ugly words. Cruel words can hurt our feelings inside, just as much as a kick or a punch hurts us on the outside.

Draw a picture of an addicted person who is really mad at someone or something else but hurts other people with ugly words and treats them in an angry way.

How do children feel when this happens?

Picture inspired by a child's drawing in *My Dad Loves Me, My Dad Has a Disease* by Claudia Black.

You Deserve The Best

Children don't deserve to be ignored or treated badly. The drug or alcohol the addicted person takes gets in the way of his love.

It stops him from showing that he cares. Instead he sometimes treats people badly or as if they don't matter.

Children can be helped if they know they are not to blame and don't deserve hurtful treatment. They must try to get help if they need it.

I'm special. I deserve to be
treated well!

It Takes Time

And remember, even when addicted people stop drinking or taking drugs, they don't change for the better right away. It takes time for their body to learn to work without drugs or alcohol.

The addicted person has to learn how to act in a caring, healthy way.

It is like learning how to ride a bike.

It takes time.

Learning to ride takes time.

Changes

Children cannot stop the addicted person from drinking or taking drugs.

But they can change themselves.

Write or **draw** about something you'd like to change about yourself.

Draw about how you would make this change.

Draw or **write** about some things you like to do.
Try to do one of these each day.

This can help children feel better.

They can enjoy themselves even if someone is addicted.

2

Feelings

Everyone Has Feelings

Feelings are not good or bad. They are just an important part of ourselves.

In families where someone drinks too much or takes drugs, the children can have a lot of uncomfortable feelings. But in these families people often don't talk about feelings.

They don't talk about the drinking or drug-taking.

Children will feel better if they pay attention to and think about their feelings.

People pay attention to their feelings when they talk, write or draw about them.

This chapter will help you think about feelings.

In some families nobody talks about feelings.

Let's Think About Uncomfortable Feelings

Anger is one uncomfortable feeling all of us have sometimes.

When some people are angry, they hurt other people.

They yell at them, call them names or stop speaking to other family members.

Sometimes when people are angry, they hurt themselves and hide their angry feelings.

Don't Lock Your Feelings Inside

When this happens, you waste energy. Your body must work hard to keep feelings locked away. This can make you feel sick and tired. You might get headaches or stomachaches or not feel very well.

It Helps To Think And Talk About Feelings

How do you feel today? _____

Some Comfortable Feelings

When do you feel:

- Happy_____
  _____

- Important _____
  _____

- Loved _____
  _____

- Comfortable _____
  _____

- Special _____
  _____

- Proud _____
  _____

Some Uncomfortable Feelings

When do you feel:

- Sad _____
  _____

- Angry _____
  _____

- Scared _____
  _____

- Worried _____
  _____

- Hurt _____
  _____

- Lonely _____
  _____

When I Am Angry?

It is okay to feel angry. All of us do sometimes.

But it is not okay to hurt other people by calling them names or hurting their bodies.

I throw stuff.

I yell and say mean
words to others.

I hurt others.

What Else Can We Do?

We Can:

- Stamp our feet

- Throw or hit a pillow

- Work off or play off our anger by doing some exercise, sport or something we like

- **Write** or **draw** or **talk** about our feelings

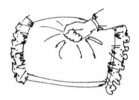

I hit a pillow!

I talk about my anger.

I ride my bike.

Anger

Have you ever seen an addicted person angry?

What did he do and how did you feel?

Once when my father was angry, he raised his fist and yelled that he was going to kill us. My father's face was scary. And I was scared.

Draw a picture of something that makes you angry.

What do you do when this happens?

I get mad when my dad does drugs, especially when he promised he'd stop.

Then I cry.

Violence

Violence sometimes comes with drug-taking.

Addicted people sometimes act in angry, out of control ways. They become scary and threaten or hurt other people in their family.

Some become violent when they are taking drugs. Others act violent when they aren't taking drugs.

This is because some people become so used to taking drugs that they feel wild and crazy without them. When this happens, they lose control of themselves and they hurt others.

It seems as if they never learned to handle problems in a non-violent way.

Draw a picture about what might happen when family members get violent and how the children feel.

Remember children do not deserve to be hurt.

Who could help children when this happens?

Help!! I'm scared!!

Picture inspired by a child's drawing in *My Dad Loves Me, My Dad Has A Disease* by Claudia Black.

Scared

Sometimes it is scary living with a person who is addicted to drugs or alcohol.

Can you think of a time when you felt scared?

Confusing

It is confusing living with someone who is addicted to drugs or alcohol.

Sometimes addicted people treat us well.

At other times the addicted person acts mean and as if he hates us.

At times we aren't sure if we love the addicted person.

We may even feel we hate him. Children feel confused when they feel love and hate for the same person. But remember, it is usually what the drugs and alcohol do to our family member that we hate.

We can still love the addicted person but hate how he behaves when he uses drugs.

But I hate the drugs he takes. They make him seem bad and mean.

Up and Down

Many people who live with an addicted family member feel as if they are on a roller coaster.

They go up and down with their feelings.

When they feel love, they are "up" and happy.

When the feel hate, they are "down" and unhappy.

Has this ever happened to you?

What makes you feel love for this person?

What makes you think that you do not like him?

It's like being on a roller coaster. Our feelings of love and hate go up and down over and over again.

Disappointment

You can't always count on an addicted person. Sometimes they let children down and embarrass and disappoint them.

Draw a picture about how an addicted person might embarrass or disappoint a child.

Has this ever happened to you?

School Concert

Inspired by a child's drawing in *My Dad Loves Me, My Dad Has A Disease* by Claudia Black

Don't Talk

Sometimes in families with an addicted member no one talks about feelings, especially uncomfortable feelings.

No one talks about the bad things that happen when a family member drinks or takes drugs.

Everyone pretends everything is okay.

If a family member drinks or takes drugs, have you ever felt you can't talk about it?

Draw or **write** about why children might find it hard to talk about their feelings or their family member's drinking and drug taking.

Nobody talks about the drug-taking. Everyone pretends everything is okay. I don't really know what is happening.

Forgetting

Sometimes children pretend they don't feel bad.

They try to forget the bad things that can sometimes happen when a family member drinks or takes drugs.

Did you ever forget something bad that happened to you?

Did you pretend it wasn't so bad?

Talk, write or **draw** a picture about it.

Once I saw my father smoking marijuana after he said he'd stopped. I pretended I didn't see, and never thought or talked about it again. Has this ever happened to you?

Guilty

Go to your room

Sometimes when my mother gets mad, I feel guilty. It seems as if I am bad and the drinking is my fault.

Picture inspired by a child's drawing in *My Dad Loves Me, My Dad Has A Disease* by Claudia Black.

Often children feel guilty and think it is their fault when a family member is addicted to drugs or alcohol.

Remember, children do not cause the addiction.

It is their parents' responsibility to stop the drug-taking. And they usually need help to do this – from a doctor or other professional.

Sometimes the addicted person blames other people, even his children, for his drinking or drug taking.

But children are never to blame. The addiction is not their fault.

Something More To Do

- Use the chart on the next page to help you draw or write about how children feel when a family member drinks or takes drugs.

- Circle some of the uncomfortable feelings you have had. Choose some to draw or write about.

- Don't forget about comfortable feelings. Put a check mark beside some of the comfortable feelings you have had.

- Draw or write about what makes you feel any of these comfortable feelings.

   And remember, do something that makes you happy everyday.

Feelings You Have Had

Check the feelings you have had below:

☐ Sad	☐ Excited
☐ Worried	☐ Upset
☐ Cozy	☐ Silly
☐ Loved	☐ Brave
☐ Loving	☐ Proud
☐ Scared	☐ Terrible
☐ Angry	☐ Terrific
☐ Special	☐ Liked
☐ Hurt	☐ Cheerful
☐ Embarrassed	☐ Depressed
☐ Disappointed	☐ Funny
☐ Happy	☐ Shy
☐ Nervous	☐ Lonely
☐ Confused	☐ Sorry

Draw, talk or **write** about times when you have had these feelings.

3

Feeling Masks

Defenses

Defenses are like masks that we wear to hide our real feelings.

Sometimes we use defenses to protect other people.

We don't want to hurt their feelings – like when someone serves us a food we don't like.

Defenses are neither bad nor good.

Sometimes we need to use them.

We don't need to share our feelings with everyone.

Not everyone is understanding.

Some people are unkind and wouldn't be good people to share feelings with.

It's Best Not To Share Feelings With A Drunk Or High Person

Sometimes it is best not to share feelings.

And nobody shares feelings all of the time.

It is best not to share feelings with drunk or high people.

Drunk or high people may get mad at you, ignore you or even forget what you said.

But it is not good to use your defenses (or masks) all of the time.

When this happens, it's like building a wall around yourself.

You are all alone and nobody can get inside.

No one will know who you are.

If you need help, no one will know that you do. They won't know what you really think or feel.

And it will be hard to make friends because people won't know the real you.

Drinking too much alcohol or taking other harmful drugs is a defense.

When addicted people take too much of a harmful drug, the drug helps to mask their uncomfortable feelings.

Then addicted people don't have to think about them.

But these uncomfortable feelings still stay deep inside.

Happy On The Outside
Sad Inside

If you hide your uncomfortable feelings – like anger, guilt and sadness – you will always have them deep inside and never be really happy.

Even though you wear your happy mask, deep down inside you will feel unhappy.

We Need To Remove Our Defenses

Defenses or feeling masks are okay. But we need to find times when we can remove them and be our true selves.

Otherwise we won't know what we really need and feel.

It is important to share our true thoughts and feelings if we want to be closer to others and find help when we need it.

Children's Defenses

Children use defenses to:

- hide their real feelings and pretend they feel okay.
- forget about the things that upset them.
- try to make others like them.
- try and stop others from getting mad at them.

Here are some defenses children use. *Circle,* some you have used.

1. Blaming other people when things go wrong.
2. Trying to please others and mostly doing what others want.
3. Being super nice and good.
4. Joking and clowning around.
5. Smiling and always acting happy and friendly.
6. Staying out of the way, being quiet and spending a lot of time alone.
7. Taking drugs.
8. Trying to be perfect and number one.
9. Telling lies.
10. Forgetting or pretending something didn't happen or it really wasn't that bad.

Defenses Or Masks Children Might Use

Fill in the defenses or masks children might use in the following situations:

1. The other children won't let them join in a game _____

_____

2. They fail a math test _____

_____

3. They didn't do their homework and the teacher gets mad _____

_____

4. They lose a new sweater at school _____

_____

5. Mom and Dad are yelling at each other _____

_____

6. They have trouble with schoolwork and the other kids tease them

_____

_____

7. Someone hits them or hurts them by saying mean things

_____

_____

8. Someone touches them in a way they don't want to be touched

_____

_____

Once my dad promised to take me to the baseball game but he didn't.

I pretended I was happy and didn't care but inside I was:

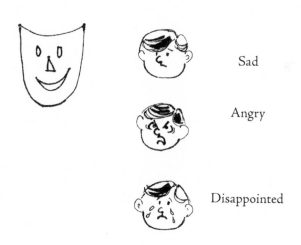

Sad

Angry

Disappointed

Draw a picture of a time you remember using a defense or mask to hide your true feelings.

Think about how you felt – disappointed, hurt, embarrassed, sad or angry?

What mask did you use to hide your feelings?

Could you have removed your mask and shown your true feelings?

Removing our masks can be hard because we are afraid.

We are afraid that we will be hurt or hurt other people or that other people won't like us if they know what we really think and feel.

I don't like it when kids are mean to me.
I don't want them to know I'm sad.
I think they'll laugh at me.

Hard To Share Feelings

You need to feel safe to remove your defenses and share your true feelings.

Draw a picture of a time when you didn't feel safe or comfortable enough to lower your defenses.

Once I was afraid to tell my father I was scared. I thought he would yell and call me a baby.

Sadness

I don't want to share when I'm sad.
It might make the
sad people I know sadder.

What Makes You Feel Good?

Think of some people who might make you feel safe so that you could lower your defenses, and share your true feelings and real self with them.

Draw them or write their names.

What makes you feel good – praise, friendship, fun?

Write and **draw** about things you can do to help you find good feelings.

And remember, defenses are okay.

But sometimes we need to remove them if we want to be close to other people and if we want to be our true selves and release uncomfortable feelings.

Thinking About The Defenses You Use

What do you do when you don't want anyone to know you feel:

1. Sad _____

_____

2. Hurt _____

_____

3. Nervous _____

_____

4. Mad _____

_____

5. Frightened _____

_____

6. Happy _____

_____

7. Worried _____

_____

8. Lonely _____

_____

Draw a picture of a mask you wear to hide your true feelings.

What feelings do you hide with this mask?

4

A Family Problem

Children Can't Stop Or Cause Addiction

Addiction is a problem children can't cause or stop.

But everyone in the family is affected when a family member is addicted to drugs.

All people act differently than how they might act if someone in the family didn't take drugs.

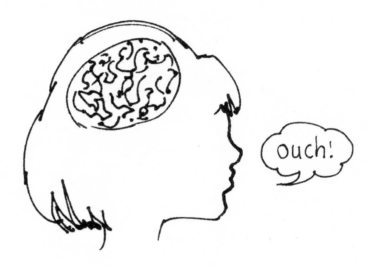

Brain

Remember when people are addicted to drugs, they don't act themselves.

The drug affects the human brain, and addicted people may act in crazy, out of control ways.

Sometimes they ignore and don't notice other people.

Can't Stop

This is because a family works a little like a mobile.

When we push one part of the mobile, all the other parts are affected and start moving too.

This happens in families.

How one family member acts affects all the others.

When family members act in healthy, balanced ways, other family members are free to act in the same way too.

It is like pushing one part of the mobile gently.

All other mobile parts move in a balanced, smooth way.

Topsy-Turvy

The addicted person doesn't always act in a healthy balanced way.

He hurts and upsets other people by ignoring them or treating them badly.

Everyone else in the family feels messed up in a tangle of uncomfortable feelings.

Some feel angry, sad and afraid.

Others feel lonely and guilty.

The addicted person is like one part of a mobile that is pushed all around and out of control.

All other mobile parts move all around and out of control too, spinning into a tangled topsy-turvy mess.

Family members become all tangled up with the addicted person – all topsy-turvy in a mess of uncomfortable feelings.

Family members often try to make things better, less confusing and more balanced.

They want to feel safe and avoid the tangled mess of uncomfortable feelings.

They want things to run smoothly, like a mobile pushed gently by the wind.

Running Smoothly

To try to keep things running smoothly, many children who live with an addicted person do some of the following things:

Don't Talk

- They don't tell anyone that their family member is addicted. It is a family secret.

- They don't talk about their feelings or experiences to other people. Sometimes it seems as if people are too busy to listen. Sometimes they are afraid that people will get angry and criticize them.

Don't Trust

- In families with addicted members, parents often break promises and disappoint the children.

- Children are afraid to trust because parents can change a lot and act in crazy, out of control ways.

Don't Feel

- They don't want to upset others with their feelings.

- They want to forget about the sad, frightening things that often happen.

Behaving in Particular Ways

Sometimes children try to make things better in their families and easier for themselves by behaving in particular ways:

Act Perfect

- They do well in school and everywhere else.

- They are helpful and try to make everyone feel better.

- They think maybe if they are good and do well, the drinking will stop, and the family will be happy.

Troublemaker

- They often act angry at others and get themselves into trouble.

- They feel angry about the drug taking. They hurt others with their anger and sometimes misbehave.

Lost Child

- They are silent and spend a lot of time alone, away from the problems of the home.

- They don't want to upset things more so they stay out of the way and keep quiet.

- They don't talk about themselves or say what they really think. They are afraid others will get mad or upset.

Clown

- They laugh, tell jokes and are fun to be with.

- They think if they can make the family laugh, they'll be happy and forget about the drug taking.

- Often those who behave like a clown have uncomfortable feelings inside.

Locked Inside a Role

All of these behaviors make sense.

They are understandable ways to cope with family problems.

Often children use more than one of these behaviors to try to help themselves and their families.

Remember, you can't control the drinking.

None of these behaviors can stop the drinking and really make things better for your family.

But sometimes children who live with addicted family members use them too much.

They get locked into these roles -- like locked into a jail.

Jail

They use them almost all the time at home with family members, or at school or other places outside the home with their friends.

When this happens, children forget to be their true selves.

They forget what they really think and feel.

They have locked their true selves, deep down, inside and far away.

Draw a picture of what happens when someone uses the same behavior almost all of the time.

Has this ever happened to you?

Breaking Out Of Roles

Children can break out of their roles like a chick breaks out of a shell.

Remember, addicted people hide their true selves behind the drugs.

Other family members sometimes hide themselves behind a role or set of behaviors they use almost all of the time.

People don't always have to hide themselves behind a role or behavior.

There are times when they can be themselves.

I'm hiding.

Perfect Person

The **Perfect Person** doesn't always have to be perfect.

Everyone makes mistakes.

It is okay when people do.

The perfect person can take time to have fun and laugh.

He doesn't always need to help other people.

He needs help himself sometimes.

Draw a picture of something the **Perfect Person** can do to escape from the perfect role he is locked into.

Everyone needs to ask for help sometimes.

Lost Child

The **Lost Child** can learn to be less alone.

He can reach out to talk and play with other people.

He can learn to say what he feels and to do what is right for him.

He doesn't have to give into other people.

Help the **Lost Child** escape from his role.

Draw some things he could do.

People don't have to stay alone to be safe.
There are people they can reach out to and
share themselves with.

Clown

The **Clown** doesn't always have to be a clown.

He can show other sides of himself.

He can be helpful, serious and smart.

He can show his sad and uncomfortable feelings too.

Draw what a child could do to unlock himself from the clown role.

It is hard work trying to keep people happy and laughing.

Clowns need a rest.

Troublemaker

The **Troublemaker** can learn to do things that get him attention in positive ways.

He can learn to have fun and get along with other people.

He can help others and try harder in school.

And he can learn to handle his anger in ways that don't get him into trouble with others.

Draw some other things the troublemaker can do.

It's no fun always being in trouble.

Non-addicted People

Not just the children act differently when a family member is addicted.

Sometimes the non-addicted parents are so upset and concerned by the drinking or drug taking that they don't always treat the children fairly.

They get angry for what seems like little or no reason. Sometimes they seem to ignore and not notice the children.

What Role Do You Play?

Act Perfect.

Children in homes with an addicted family member need to find times when they can escape from their roles.

If you play one of these roles, make a pact with yourself to do this.

Lost Child

Circle the family role you think you play the most often.

Draw or *write* about times when you can try to break out of this role.

Remember, you cannot make the drug abuser better.

Trouble-
maker

But you can change yourself.

Can You Be Your Self?

In healthy families children can be their true selves.

Clown.

They can feel comfortable telling people what they think and feel.

And they don't have to try to make everyone feel better by being funny or perfect.

They don't have to stay out of the way to feel safe.

They don't need to make trouble to find attention.

5

Help Yourself

What Can You Change?

Sometimes children feel unhappy about how things are in their family.

I hate it when my parents fight.

Draw a picture of something a child might wish could be different in his family.

Is this something children can change?

Yelling! Shouting! Screaming!

Children need to know there are many things they can't change.

They can't stop the drinking or drug taking. They can't stop their parents from fighting.

They can't really make things better for other family members who spend time worrying about the addicted person.

Children must decide what things they can change and what things they can't. It is a waste of time and energy to worry about things you can't change.

I wish I could stop the drug -- taking!!

Remember, it is a waste of time to worry about things you cannot change.

Sometimes children worry so much about the addicted person and their other family members who seem sad, angry and unhappy that they forget to have fun and enjoy their lives.

Children who take care of themselves learn to stop worrying about the things they can't change.

It is a waste of time that could be spent enjoying their lives.

Problems and Worries

Everyone has problems and worries. What do you worry about when you think about:

1. Your family_____

   _____

2. Your dad_____

   _____

3. Your mom_____

   _____

4. Your brothers and sisters_____

   _____

5. Your friends_____

   _____

6. School_____

   _____

7. What is your biggest problem or worry?_____

   _____

8. Do you have any others?_____

   _____

9. What problem can you let go of and let other people worry about?

   _____

Coping with Uncomfortable Feelings

Children take care of themselves when they learn to handle uncomfortable feelings.

Sometimes children feel hurt and angry about some of the things family members do when they drink or take drugs.

Sometimes children feel hurt and angry because the addicted person gets all the attention, and nobody pays much attention to them.

Children feel unhappy when they hang onto uncomfortable feelings and keep them stuffed inside.

Think of ways to cope with uncomfortable feelings.

Do What Feels Right for You

Children take care of themselves when they say no to someone who wants them to do something that isn't good for them or might hurt them.

Can you *draw* a picture of something children should say no to if they want to take care of themselves?

The Whole Wheel

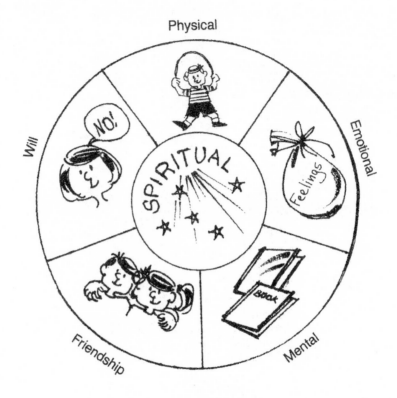

Based on the Whole Wheel Circle outlined in *Choicemaking* by Sharon We-gscheider-Cruise.

Children who want to take care of themselves need to pay attention to all of the areas shown in the circle or the Whole Wheel.

All of these areas are the parts that make up the kind of people we are.

Take Care Of Every Part of Yourself

Sometimes children only take care of themselves in some of these areas.

They might work hard and do well in school but forget to have fun with their friends.

This means only taking care of small pieces of yourself and forgetting about all the rest.

This is as if some parts of the circle are empty.

And children who ignore some of these areas might feel empty too.

Draw or **write** about some of the good things you do to take care of yourself in these areas.

Put a star beside the areas where you take good care of yourself.

Put an X beside the areas where you need to take better care of yourself.

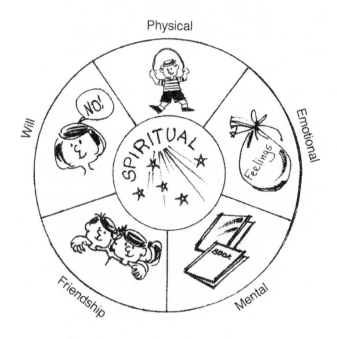

Questions based on the Whole Wheel model
described in *Another Chance* by Sharon Wegscheider-Cruise.

Areas Where You Need to Spend More Time

How could you take better care of yourself in some of the areas where you need to spend more time?

The questions below will help you.

- **Physical** -- Do you appreciate your body? Do you take care of it by eating properly and getting plenty of rest and exercise?

- **Mental** -- Do you like learning? Do you work hard to learn? Do you like using your own ideas and creating new projects?

- **Will** -- Do you make good decisions? Can you plan and set goals for yourself? Do you do what feels best for your-self and not just what you think others want?

- **Emotions** -- Do you think about and find ways to express your feelings? Can you share your feelings with others? Do you handle your anger in a way that doesn't hurt you or other people?

- **Social** -- Do you spend some of your time with other people? Do you enjoy the company of others? Do you have friends? Can you keep friends?

- **Spiritual** -- Do you remember that you are special and that you have a special place in this world? Do you take time to be alone and to think about and enjoy the wonders of our world?

Something More to Do

Everyone has problems. They are just part of life. Sometimes we can solve problems. At other times new ones come our way. Some problems are harder to solve. They don't always go away.

But all of us can learn to handle problems in a healthier way.

To handle problems in a healthy way means to cope.

When you learn to cope with family problems you take good care of yourself.

You Can Cope with Problems!

Let's think about problems children sometimes have.

Problem 1

Feeling all alone and as if you don't matter. This can happen when:

- Family members are too busy or spend all their time worrying about the addicted person and ignore the children.

- Family members are so tired because of worrying about the addicted person that they act crabby and angry with the children.

- The addicted person takes drugs which get in the way of his love and he ignores or treats the children badly.

What Can Children Do?

Poor Solutions:

- Yell at and treat other people badly.

- Refuse to help around the house or do your homework.

Good Solutions:

- Share your feelings with others.

- Ask for what you need to make you feel better like a hug, a cuddle, a pat on the back or someone to spend time with you, perhaps playing a game.

Other Solutions:

Problem 2

Feeling forced to take sides. This can happen when family members say angry, unkind things about other family members. Children feel bad when this happens because they usually care about all family members. It is upsetting to hear unkind things said about people we care about.

What Can Children Do?

Poor Solutions:

- Listen and keep hurt feelings inside.

- Pretend it doesn't matter and let the other person keep on saying unkind things.

Good Solutions

- Tell the family member you feel hurt when they say unkind things about another family member. Ask them to talk about something else.

Other Suggestions:

I feel in the middle.
Whose side am I on?

Problem 3

When parents fight, children often feel scared, lonely and angry.

What Can Children Do?

Poor Solutions:

- Listen and worry.

Good Solutions:

- Go for a bike ride or a walk. Listen to music or watch TV.

- Don't get involved. It is your parents' problem.

- Play a game or read.

Other Suggestions:

I don't know what to do when
my parents fight.

Problem 4

Feeling afraid of a family member: This often happens with addicted people. They might yell a lot, say cruel things and hurt other people. **No child deserves to be hurt.** If a family member frightens you or is about to hurt you or anyone else, there are things you can do.

What Can Children Do?

Good Solutions:

- Call or go to a relative's, friend's or the police or another caring adult.

- Know your emergency number and call for help.

Other Suggestions:

I might be hurt.
What should I do?

Problem 5

Feeling afraid to drive with a family member who is drunk or taking drugs.

What Can Children Do?

Poor Solutions:

- Go with the family member.

Good Solutions:

- Tell the high or drunk person you're not going.

- Know the phone number of someone else you can call -- a neighbor, a friend or another family member. Tell them your problem and ask them for a ride home.

- Talk to a teacher or call the police. Tell them why you are worried and ask for help.

Other Solutions:

Think about a problem you or another child might want to learn to cope with better.

Draw a picture about the problem and a healthy way to cope with this problem.

Remember, you can take good care of yourself and have a happier life even if someone in your family is addicted to drugs.

Draw or *write* about some of the things you plan to do to take better care for yourself.

Should I drive with my dad when he is drunk???

6

Decisions

Each One Of Us Is Special

We all look different and have different talents, interests and things that make us happy.

Thinking About How You Are Special

- What makes you feel special?_____

  _____

- What do you like doing?_____

  _____

- What do you do well?_____

  _____

- What do you think other people like about you?_____

  _____

- What do you like about yourself?_____

  _____

- What are some of the things that make you feel proud?

  _____

I'm a fast runner. I'm good at drawing. I'm proud of myself.

Look After Yourself

Sometimes when a parent is addicted to drugs, children have to take good care of themselves. The addicted parent is so involved with his drugs that he can't be a good parent to the children. The non-addicted parent may be too worried and distracted to notice the children. Sometimes children just have to be good parents to themselves.

Circle the decisions below that show children can take good care of themselves.

- You decide not to eat breakfast and you are hungry all morning at school.

- You stayed up late and you are tired all day at school.

- You said no to a friend who asked you to smoke a cigarette.

- You shared a hard to share feeling with someone with whom you felt safe.

Think about the decisions you make that show you care about you.

What about decisions that weren't so good for you?

Do you sometimes feel that you have to parent yourself, that there is no one to take good care of you?

Draw or *write* about a time when you felt this way.

Thinking About Others

Good decisions also show that you're concerned about other people. It is important to think about the effects of your decisions upon others and to show that you respect them and their feelings.

Which of the following decisions show consideration for others?

- You turn off the lights and the TV when you finish using them.

- People are making fun of a classmate because he doesn't do well in school. You tell them to stop and ask your classmate to play.

- Your brother makes you mad. You want to kick him but you don't.

- Your mother is carrying heavy groceries. You pretend you don't see her so you don't have to help.

- You finish eating some popcorn on the way to school. You drop the empty bag on the ground.

Think about some other decisions that show you care about people.

Have you ever been hurt by a decision that someone else made? Did you feel that they didn't care about you or respect your feelings? *Draw* or *write* about this.

I pick up my clothes so that others won't trip over them.

Sometimes decisions are difficult and scary to make.

Think of a big decision you had to make. What did you do and how did you feel?

Was it the best decision for you?

Draw or *write* about it.

Once when I was afraid of my dad
I called the police.

Everyday Decisions

Think of some decisions you make each day:

- In the morning _____

  _____

- With your family _____

  _____

- During school _____

_____

- After school _____

_____

- At home _____

_____

- With friends _____

_____

- By yourself _____

_____

Grown-Up Decisions

What decisions will you make as you grow older?

- When you're a teenager _____

_____

- When you're an adult _____

_____

Which decisions will you make with other people?

Which decisions will affect other people?

I was so happy when my hockey team won. I decided to share this happy feeling with my brother.

Making Decisions

Making good decisions is not always easy. When making a decision, it sometimes helps to go through the following steps:

1. The Problem

2. What choices you have?

   (a) _____

   (b) _____

   (c) _____

3. What might happen with these choices and how do you feel about each one?

         Consequences   **Feelings**

   (a) _____

   (b) _____

   (c) _____

4. What is the best decision and why? _____

_____

Using The Steps To Help Us Make Good Decisions

Let's use the steps to help us make good decisions. Choose a problem and see if the steps can help you.

- Your friends dare you to go into an abandoned building.

- Your friends are smoking. They try to give you a cigarette. You feel left out but you don't want to smoke. What should you do?

- You are afraid to drive with your parent who has been drinking. What should you do?

Think of a problem that worries you. **Draw** or **write** about it and some good choices you could make to solve it.

I worry about getting hit when my dad is drunk.

What can you do?

- Go next door.

- Call the police.

- Find a safe place to go.

- Go for a walk.

Every day there are pressures on us to make decisions.

The following things might affect your decisions:

1. Yourself – what you think, feel and value.

2. What others think.

3. Your parents.

4. Teachers and other important adults.

5. Television programs, commercials and movies.

6. Anything else you can think of?_____

_____

Look at the factors listed above. Think about which ones might affect the following choices.

Write its number beside each choice. Remember more than one factor can affect each choice.

Food I eat _____   Books, TV programs and movies
My behavior _____   that I enjoy _____
My friends _____   _____

Hairstyle and clothing   Clubs and activities I join
_____   _____

My schoolwork _____ Feelings I share _____

Courage

We want to be liked by other people.

Sometimes other children put pressure on us to make decisions. This is called peer pressure.

Other children may try to get us to do things that aren't good for us.

Children might want to say no to their friends but it is hard to say no if children think the other kids won't like them.

It's hard to say no to the others. You have to be brave to do it.

Advertisements

Commercials and other advertisements try to persuade us to buy things.

Some commercials tell us to drink beer.

They make it seem that drinking beer will make us happy.

We will have lots of friends and fun.

We need to think for ourselves and not let commercials make decisions for us.

Has a commercial ever influenced your decision?

Beer isn't always fun.

Parents Are Teachers

Often children grow up to do many of the same things their parents did.

This can happen even when children say they'll never be like their parents.

This is because children learn from their parents.

When they watch their parents, they learn how adults act.

Children who don't spend a lot of time with other adults, learn the most about how adults act from their parents.

Parents are teachers too.

A New Way

If someone's parents are addicted to drugs, children might not learn any other way to solve problems.

They might hide their feelings behind drugs because they never learned any other way.

But children don't have to grow up to be just like their parents.

They can learn to make healthy decisions and say **no** to too much alcohol and harmful drugs.

Children can learn a new way.

Getting Help

Children can learn to take better care of themselves.

They can say no to drugs and learn to handle feelings and cope with problems in a healthy way. Children are not alone.

They can find people to help them, people they can share their feelings and problems with.

Ask For What You Need

Children need to ask for what they need.

Think of people who can help:

- when you feel lonely and sad.
- when you want to play a game and have some fun.
- when the other kids pick on you.
- when you're afraid that someone will hurt you.
- when you are sick.
- when you have trouble with your schoolwork.

Remember you can't always choose what happens to you but you can choose how you act.

You could make decisions that show you care about yourself and others.

When people make fun of my dad, I can choose to walk away and not fight. I can find something to do that I enjoy.

A neighbor can sometimes help with the problem. If she can't who else could?

Remember to ask for what you need.

You won't get everything you ask for but you'll feel better for asking.

Not everyone will be able to help.

Keep trying. You'll find someone.

Draw a picture about a time when you wanted to ask for what you needed. What happened?

Good Things About You

Circle the words below that are good things about you.

They will help you remember that you are special and deserve the best.

Make good decisions for yourself.

- Artistic
- Gentle
- Friendly
- Imaginative
- Humorous
- Caring
- Intelligent
- Creative
- Good decision maker
- Considerate

- Patient
- Brave
- Musical
- Responsible
- Independent
- Athletic
- Kind
- Truthful
- Shares feelings

Anything else? _____

_____

_____

Family Change

There Are Many Different Kinds of Families

Some families are large. Some are small.

Some children live with both parents.

Others live with just one parent. And sometimes children have stepbrothers and stepsisters.

There is no right kind of family.

All families are okay.

Draw a picture about your family.

Sometimes children think that their family is the only one with problems. But every family has problems.

Some families handle problems in a healthier way than others -- by talking them through, sharing feelings, making plans and comforting each other.

Children who feel unhappy about their family problems may wish they lived in another family.

Draw a picture of your dream family -- the kind you might like to live with.

How would the parents in your dream family act?

How would it be different for the children?

Families Can Learn To Get Along Better

Some families have the problem of addiction.

Family members with this problem can't stop taking their drug.

Remember, children do not cause the addiction and can't make the addicted person better.

But things can still improve in families even if someone is addicted to drugs.

Families can learn to handle problems in a healthy way and grow closer to each other.

Rules

All families have rules but sometimes in a home with an addicted family member the rules become confusing and change from day to day.

This happens when people take drugs and behave differently than they do when they aren't taking drugs.

Do the rules in your house change and confuse you?
What rules do you think are okay? What rules would you like to change?

If you could make the rules, what rules would you make?

I make my bed.

Sometimes it seems like there is a rule never to talk about the drinking or drug taking and the bad things that can happen.

Complaints

It is hard to live with addicted family members.

Some children who do complain about:

1. Little family fun.
2. Family fighting (name calling, criticism, putdowns).
3. Little attention from parents.
4. No one to talk to.
5. Doing all the work.
6. Everyone in the family being alone and separate.
7. Never being able to be natural or silly.
8. Always doing what others want -- no one asks what you want.
9. Working hard to keep the addict from getting mad.
10. A sad, angry non-addicted parent.
11. Confusion -- parenting behavior and rules change.
12. The "No Talk" rule.

Circle the things that you think are true in your family.
Write or **draw** about any of them.

Sometimes it seems as if we never laugh or have fun.

Good Times

But there can still be good things about families when someone is addicted to drugs.

I like it when we go to McDonald's.

Draw a picture about what you like best about your family.

Family Closeness

Even when someone is addicted to drugs, families can learn to be happier and closer to each other.

Who do you feel close to in your family? What makes you feel close?

Is there someone you'd like to be closer to? What makes it hard for you to be close to this person?

I feel close to my sister.

Families can help children feel cared for and special. Have you ever felt this way in your family?

Draw or *Write* about what makes you feel this way.

I feel special on my birthday.

Let's think about brothers and sisters.

What is good about having them?

What makes them seem like a nuisance?

If you are an only child, what do you like about this? What don't you like?

Sometimes brothers and sisters fight a lot or ignore each other. When this happens, everyone just feels lonelier and sadder, but brothers and sisters can work together to make family life friendlier or more fun.

They can play a game and talk about their day and share their feelings with each other.

Think about your brothers and sisters. Can you share feelings or experiences with them? What would make it easier for you to do this?

We can share feelings.

If you don't have brothers or sisters, think about other family members you could get closer to.

How about cousins, aunts, uncles or grandparents?

Or what about children or adult friends?

How could you do this?

I have someone to play with.

Sharing Feelings

Sometimes, when someone is addicted, family members forget to share feelings.

Choose a feeling you would like to share with a family member.

- Sad
- Scared

- Mad
- Hurt

- Proud
- Excited

- Happy
- Lonely

Draw about what you think would happen if you shared this feeling. What would you like to happen?

Can you help other family members to share feelings with you?

What about the happenings in your day? Can you share these with your family? Do you feel that they are interested? What makes you feel this way?

Think about something either terrific or horrible that happened to you. Were you able to share this experience with someone?

Good Things About Family Members

Draw or **write** about what you like about each of your family members.

What is good about you? You are important too. All of us need to feel good about ourselves.

Compliment your family members. Tell them what makes you feel good about them.

And don't forget to say something good to yourself everyday.

My father takes me
to hockey games.

My brother is funny
and lots of fun.

My mother gives me ice cream
and ginger ale
when I'm sick.

How Could You Make Someone in Your Family Feel Special?

Try to plan some fun with your family this week.

Can you ask your family to join in with you?

Draw a picture of what it might be.

I'm going to play a game with my family.

Lots of Kids Like Us

Feeling Alone

Sometimes when children live with an addicted family member, they feel all alone, as if they don't matter. When people are high or drunk, they don't notice the children and sometimes they treat the children badly. Other family members are upset by the drug -- taking and may forget to notice the children too.

Sometimes family members who worry about the drug-taking are irritated and angry, and say unkind things to the children. They forget to remind the children how important and special they are.

When children are ignored, they may feel alone, even in their own families.

I'm not like the others. I don't like what they're doing anyway.

Children may feel alone, in their classrooms, or even when playing with other children.

They may find it hard to feel part of a group.

They might feel different and think they're the only ones who have an addicted family member.

Reasons For Feeling Alone

Children give the following reasons for feeling alone and not part of the group:

- Nobody likes me.

- I'd rather be alone.

- I don't like what the others are doing.

- I'm not important.

Have you ever had any of these feelings?

Circle those that you have or **write** about a time when you felt any of these ways.

When children feel they are different, they sometimes spend a lot of time alone.

They may be very quiet in class and in other groups, and may not talk or share their thoughts with others.

They may act out, be silly and goofy and do crazy things to get attention from others.

Maybe others will notice them and think they are cool. Maybe then they can become part of the group.

There are children with addicted family members all over the world.

Lots of Kids

It's hard to feel different, and not part of the group. Everyone feels that way sometimes.

But children with addicted family members are not alone.

There are lots of other children just like them.

People believe that in a classroom of 25 children, there may be five or six who have an addicted parent.

That's a lot of children.

But most of these children don't know about each other.

That's because they don't talk about a family member's addiction to each other.

Sometimes children don't even know their parents are addicted because no one at home talks about it.

Help For Family Members

There are Alateen and Al-Anon meetings to help other family members.

Lots of people have the problem of addiction.

When addicted people decide to get better, there are many places to get help.

Some ask for help at a hospital or treatment center.

Some go to AA meetings.

In AA people with the problem of addiction help themselves and each other by talking about their drug taking and working together to try and stay sober.

Has anyone in your family gone to a treatment center or AA to get help?

Family members do not have to be all alone and confused. They can share feelings and learn to feel better at these meetings.

After Drug - Taking Has Stopped

Don't forget, even if the family member has stopped the drug taking, things don't always get better right away. It takes time for people to learn how to act differently after the drug taking has stopped.

And even after the addicted person has stopped taking drugs, he might start doing drugs all over again.

But many addicted people do get better.

Families can learn to feel closer and happier.

No matter what happens, you can take care of yourself and have a happier life.

Has anyone in your family stopped the drug taking?

How did you feel when this happened?

Did anything change or do things seem the same or even worse?

Lots of kids feel confused and worried when a family member stops taking his drug.

It takes a long time for children to trust the addicted person. They wonder if he will start drinking all over again or if he will suddenly change and seem cruel and mean or ignore them.

Children may feel hopeful and happy that the drug taking has stopped, but worry that it will start all over again.

I'm still worried. What's going to happen?

Afraid To Bring Friends Home

Sometimes children with addicted family members are afraid to bring friends home.

All children want to be proud of their families.

But it can be embarrassing when a family member is drunk.

Then children can feel ashamed of their families and afraid to invite friends over.

Has this ever happened to you?

How can children feel more comfortable about inviting friends to be with them?

- Can you talk to your non-addicted parent or an adult friend about the problem?

- Could they help you come up with a plan?

- Could they be there to help you when your friend comes over?

- Could they take you and your friend out to dinner and a movie?

- If kids make fun of your addicted parent you may feel upset and hurt. But remember, addiction is your parents' responsibility. You can't stop or cause the addiction. Maybe you could explain the problem to your friends.

Learn To Be Part of a Group

Children who feel alone can learn to be part of a group.

They can begin to share their ideas with others.

They can listen when others speak and try not to disrupt the group by being silly or noisy and doing crazy things.

Here are some groups, some children belong to.

Put a check mark beside the group you belong to:

___ Church Groups   ___ Team Sports

___ School   ___ After school lessons

___ Cubs/Brownies   ___ Scouts/Guides.

Any others? _____
_____

Which group would you like to belong to? _____
_____

I would like to belong to a hockey team.

I'm part of my class at school.

I would like to join after-school Art.

Even when you want to be with others, some children might not let you play.

This happens to all children sometimes.

Kids aren't always kind to each other.

And nobody is liked by everyone.

When this happens, you can be your own best friend, and find something you enjoy doing by yourself.

All Kinds Of Friends

Friends don't always have to be your own age.

Friends can be much older or younger than you.

Friends are people who care about you and people you like, can have fun with and talk to about the good and bad happenings in your life.

Friends are all different.

Some are good to play with and others to share your feelings with.

You can make friends right in your own family, with a brother, a sister or a parent. How about cousins, aunts or uncles?

Some people are happy with one or two friends.

Others like to have many.

Draw a picture about some or one of your friends.

I have a few friends.

Younger people can
be friends too.

My grandfather is a
friend to me.

I have lots of friends.

**There are lots of different kinds of friends. Some are old,
some are young. Some people have a few friends.
Some have lots.**

Even a pet can be a friend.

When some children feel lonely, they enjoy talking to, cuddling
or playing with a pet.

Do you have a pet who can be a friend to you?

People Who Are Part Of Your Life

Write the names of the people who are part of your life and who you interact and communicate with.

Put the important people or the people you see most often in the first circle.

Put the others in the *second circle*.

In the *third circle add* the people you see, just some of the time.

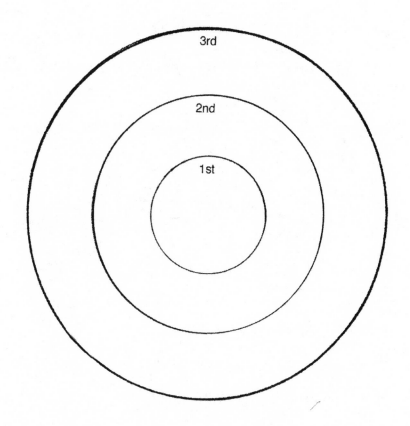

Be a Good Friend to Yourself

To be a good friend and to have others like you, you have to be a good friend to yourself.

Don't forget to find things you like about yourself.

Say something good to yourself each day.

If you don't like yourself, you can't expect other people to like you.

What good things can you say to yourself each day?

Circle The Things That Show You How You Care About Yourself:

- You say something good to yourself each day.

- You ask for help when you need it.

- You feel all your feelings.

- You choose to share some of your feelings with others.

- You find times when you can be yourself when you don't have to wear a defense mask and get locked into a behavior.

- You remember that you are not to blame for your family member's addiction and you can't make the addicted person better.

- You try to stop worrying about the things you can't change.

- You try to have fun everyday by doing something you enjoy.

- You make decisions that are good for you.

- You say no to things you feel aren't right for you.

- You join a group where you and other family members learn about addiction.

- You learn to cope with problems.

- You make sure you have a balance in your life -- you take care of yourself in all of the important areas.

Bibliography

I am indebted to the following works as sources for this book. I hope they will assist others.

Ackerman, Robert. **Children of Alcoholics: A Guidebook for Educators, Therapists and Parents.** Holmes Beach, Florida, Learning Pub. 1978.

Black, Claudia. **It Will Never Happen to Me.** Denver, CO: Medical Administration, 1982.

_____**My Dad Loves Me, My Dad Has A Disease.** Denver, CO: Medical Administration, 1979.

Children Are People Support Group Training Manual. St. Paul, MN: CAP Inc., 1985 (rev).

Cork, M.R. **The Forgotten Children.** Toronto, Canada: Addiction Research Foundation, 1969.

Hastings, Jill and Typpo, Marion. **An Elephant in the Living Room: The Children's Book.** Minneapolis, MN: Comp Care, 1984.

Panzica, N. **Your Teen and Drugs.** Toronto, Canada: McGraw-Hill Ryerson, 1983.

Wegscheider-Cruse, Sharon. **Choice-Making.** Pompano Beach, Florida: Health Communications, 1985.

Wegscheider-Cruse, Sharon. **Another Chance: Hope And Health For The Alcoholic Family.** Palo Alto, CA: Science and Behavior, 1981.

Bio

Dr. O'Connor is a psychologist who practices in Toronto, Ontario. She has written I Can Be Me to support children of alcoholic parents. I Can Be Me provides parents, family members and helping professionals with a comprehensive, yet easy to implement resource to help children of alcoholic parents. She also consults and conducts workshops with organizations and professionals about a range of topics, including How to Help Children of Alcoholic Parents.

Dr. O'Connor can be reached at:

E-mail: dsoconnor@solutionsforchildproblems.com
Website: www.solutionsforchildproblems.com